Phoenix Rising Above The Ashes

My Story Of Restoration

by

Crystal Corbin

Contents

Foreword

Are you stagnant? Have you plateaued? Are you capable of producing more than what you are? Are you being challenged? Do you even desire to be? Are you too comfortable for the demands of your purpose?

What do you need to do? What conversations do you need to have? What amount of pressure needs to be applied to you for the sake of your purpose?

A distracted person is defenseless against the wiles of the adversary. Once focused, one can administrate, steward and direct his energies towards areas, that otherwise lay waste and deformed. The adequate use of stamina in the direction most necessary, is a powerful way to assure that the purposes of God for a life, time and moment are birthed accurately. Traps, snares, and devices of hell against you, your purpose and future, are activated once you are looking in a direction where you shouldn't be. Being distracted is the way that most attempts from hell against you are successful. Being alert, sober and watchful, and turned in the right direction, is a powerful way to maintain a God-view and perspective that is not intimidated by opposing forces.

FOCUS- It is the only way to fulfill your purpose and to galvanize the resources needed for your assignment. Be cognitive, alert, sober, vigilant, detecting and perceptive! Protect your focus; if you do that well, you'll have a purpose!

Crystal has given a blueprint for handling purpose. Your purpose is entirely Prophetic. This is not just a book; this is a prophetic word for your life.

Ecclesiastes 10:10 (NET) "If an iron axhead is blunt and a workman does not sharpen its edge, he must exert a great deal of effort; so wisdom has the advantage of giving success."

The problem in many areas, whether with individuals, ministries, businesses or ideas, with regard to the lack of consistent success, is the lack of sharpened axes in their lives. There are some voices that are gifted with an abrasive mantle and purpose whose function is to sharpen those around them to bring the wisdom that leads to success. Some of us are too soft for success, and this is why we settle for leading ourselves, we cannot handle the strength of an axe, falling to the root of our low productivity. You need an AXE in your life. An Axe must be, Precise, Accurate, Discerning, Perceptive but strong, abrasive and intolerant of devices of the devil or issues in the character that prevents the God-kind of success in you! If you want success, you need an AXE. Someone must be responsible for sharpening you.

THIS BOOK IS THAT!

- JEREMIAH DANIEL DAVIS

Introduction

In this book we will look at Esther's life and how God used her life to push me into destiny. We will look at her life - long before she became a Queen. She had to go through a beautification process before she was selected as Queen. Many people look at Esther only as a Queen that prospered, but many forget about the losses, struggles, hurts and pain that she went through to get to the palace. Her pain was a process to prepare her for the palace. She became a leader for her people because she had been prepared through her pain.

We understand loss and pain and we do not want others to experience the same loss. Esther experienced the loss of her parents and the pain of death. Esther was catapulted into her destiny and purpose because she was willing to sacrifice herself to save others. She was not only a Queen but a woman who was able to speak influentially and shift atmospheres. When she trusted God and put everything on the line, she was exalted to a place of power, position, and influence.

We will also look at how God uses the most painful experiences in our lives (ashes) and restores us and redeems us to a point that we can fly away into our purpose and destiny like a Phoenix.

What is God trying to shift you into and use to prosper you in this season?

Chapter 1: The Process

Many people look at Esther and focus mainly on her time when she was prosperous and a Queen. Many times, her struggle is not represented. We forget that she had experienced pain and had to go through an internal and external beautification process. Many also think that the process happened overnight and that it did not take time. I too experienced a beautification process of my own that God took me through.

God has truly shifted my brokenness to beauty. He used my pain to catapult me into becoming a woman who can shift atmospheres. I was broken by many experiences in my life. He used those experiences to heal me and to catapult me into destiny by assisting other people, by telling my own story and by my faith walk. My faith journey has been one of pain, pressure, insecurity, depression, and anxiety. My life has now become a transition of healing, power, exultation, faith, marriage, ministry, overall growth, and progress.

The process of beautification is to get rid of the toxins and to go through the process with God. This is when something beautiful is created. My process began when I started to prepare for my future spouse. I wanted a spouse for many years. I had been looking for love in all the wrong places and for all the wrong reasons. I wanted a husband to affirm me and confirm that I was valued, and I had purpose. I thought that I had it all together and that I just needed someone to love me, but I never realized that I needed to love myself and experience how God loves me. When looking for love, validation and pleading with God for a husband, I had a rude awakening! God said that He could not give me a husband, because I would break him!

This caused me to realize that bitterness had been lying dormant in my heart. I had experienced loss and resentment from failed relationships, even a failed engagement, that I let fester in my heart. I began to see that I was not as nice and kind as I thought I was. I allowed pain to overtake who I was, and pain was who I had become. I began to realize that I was hiding my pain and pretending to be okay. This led to a toxic heart that was full of bitterness and resentment. The way that I began to guard my heart was by being mean to people and by pushing them away. I would push them away so that I was no longer able to feel the hurt, not realizing that I was hurting others around me. I had heard that statement that *"hurt people hurt people,"* but today, I am walking in redemption.

"Redeemed people also redeem people."

Redemption is a process, but every day I choose to walk in healing and redemption, and I know I am healed and redeemed in Christ. Each time I try to help others be redeemed and walk in who and what God has called them to be, it brings another level of healing and another level of beautification and purification. As I give from my place of pain, suffering, loss, and experience, the more I walk closely with God in my purpose.

Esther risked everything in her life to become a savior to her people. She trusted God and began to have blind faith even if it were inconvenient and could cost her life. Most people do not have blind faith to trust God to the point of risking their lives. What are you willing to sacrifice for you to be able to save someone else? Is your life more important to you, or will you lay down your life? Is your comfort more important, or are you willing to be uncomfortable and sacrifice for the oil to be pressed out of you? I have been tried and tested in my comfort. When I was willing to be tested, lose things, sacrifice, and be pruned and uncomfortable, it led to my healing, deliverance, and blessings. When I lost everything that I had used to define my life; and when I became obedient and placed my faith in God, I was able to redefine who I was. When you are defined, affirmed, and validated in God, that is when you truly know who you are. Amid pressure, you will discover who you truly are and what you truly believe and how much you truly love God.

Imagine this, Esther heard of the plot for her people to be killed. Feeling the pressure of her true identity being found out, and worried for her own life and her people's lives, she decided to go forward and believe what God said. She was stuck between a rock and a hard place. Can you imagine the level of fear that she was facing? She did not put her trust in herself, but instead she put her trust in Yahweh. She trusted the direction and path that He would place her in. She decided to do a three-day fast to confirm the direction of how to save her people. Who are you called to save? Are you willing to seek God under pressure for direction and understanding on why you are experiencing it and where it is taking you? Just like a bow and arrow, the pressure is not there to break you. It is there to catapult you forward into the direction that God is trying to take you. What you might feel is holding you back, might be catapulting you into destiny. You need to look at yourself from the right perspective. You need to begin to see yourself the way that God sees you. You see yourself in pain, but God sees you in the palace. He will see you in the palace long before you can imagine yourself there.

We must understand that there is a process that will get you to where you need to be. He will allow those things that felt like they were going to burn and debilitate you to push you into purpose and allow you to soar. Soon, others will see that we can be redeemed and soar further than we ever dreamed.

A Phoenix is a mythical creature that is burned, and although it dies, it can be restored and come back to life. This is the heart that God has for His people – that they will go through circumstances, but they will be restored, and they will not look like what they have been through. There are many examples in the Bible where people experienced suffering and pain, but after their processes they were even more prosperous. We see this in the story of Job. He experienced much loss, but after the process he was blessed twofold. As we have gone through the Global Pandemic of 2020, we all have experienced much loss and might even wonder, *"Where is God?"* We must realize that God can work through this and bless His people if they are willing to be tried and processed knowing that there is even more for them on the other side. I have been more blessed in the time where there has been great loss. If you are willing to trust the process in everything, you will be able to see God in the process, and you will see the purpose of it. It will be reminder of **Romans 8:28 (KJV)** *"that all things work together for good to them that love God..."* Even in this time, I have seen that many have experienced loss; yet still many have said that this has been a year of prosperity. They have been able to work on the things that led them to purpose as the whole world had been forced to slow down. In my own personal life, I was able to focus on my book and the things that God had called me to do. I began to realize that my current job was not leading me towards my purpose and destiny, and it was keeping me from the things that God had called me to be. I am now launching out in faith to succeed in these things with much prayer and direction from God. God even took my job and schooling away from me, which gave me time to focus on the things that God was asking of me and not be stuck in my own thought process. Instead, I am following the guidance of where God is taking me, though unfamiliar.

The process for Esther's beautification was at least a year long. It was six months of purification with oil and myrrh, six months with sweet odors, and with other things for the purifying of women **(Esther 2:12 KJV)**. Esther was described as *"fair and beautiful"* **(v. 7)** before she even went through her beautification and purification process. God will see us as beautiful even when we are only able to see pain and brokenness. God sees us as a beautiful creation, even when we are filthy as rags. We can be beautiful and still need to go through a purification process. When I was living in a place of pain, I did not see the true state I was in because I only saw the beauty. I did not recognize the pain. When God exposed my brokenness, I began to see that I needed to experience a beautification process. The process was needed and led to my metamorphosis into inner beauty and knowing who I truly was. When I was able to go through this process, I began to see that for many years my identity was wrapped up in pain and not truly who God had called me to be.

The enemy wants us to doubt who we are. He wants us to be defined by the pain, struggle, and bad experiences in our life to determine who we are. In Esther's life she could have been hesitant about who she was. She could have thought, *"I have lost so much in life. I do not have parents. I am a Jew, and I am from a disliked nation. Why would the King choose me?"* In my own life I felt abandoned by my father and by the men in my life. I felt unloved. I had many relationships where I was mistreated and abused. At the time, I did not realize that these issues were occurring because of my own expectations, what I said to myself and others, and my mindset. I allowed these situations in my life.

Just as Satan misconstrued and deceived Eve to make her think that she was not like God and she was missing out on something - although Eve was already like God and was able to distinguish between good and evil - I also thought that I was not worthy of love, did not have great purpose, and that God could not use me. All the time when I was believing the lie that I was not worthy, God was whispering that He loved me, I had purpose, He had created me from the foundations of the Earth, and I was fearfully and wonderfully made. I did not realize that my own broken mindset kept me in a broken state and allowed others to treat me the way they did. When a Queen recognizes her status and authority, people will respect and honor her position and authority.

When you know who you are and whose you are, walk in the authority that God has given you. You recognize that you have royalty in your bloodline, and you are royalty. When you become accustomed to what you are and whose you are, you will begin to esteem yourself in a different perspective and light. Esther had to go through the process of seeing herself as an orphan with no family aside from Mordecai, her cousin. Once she started the process of purification, she probably felt unworthy of the purification and beautification, but after a while it became part of her routine and she became familiar with the ways of the palace. God wants us to be washed and purified in Him. He does this with His loving words. He washed me with His Word, and He began to remind me of who He said I was through the Word that He gave me. At first it felt strange to be treated with love, respect, and as someone that was deserving of God's time and true friendship. During this time God sent a few selective people to stand by my side throughout my purification process.

This is observed through Esther's process. She was assigned handmaidens who walked her through preparation for purification. God will assign people to your life who will recognize that you need to be cleaned up and will stand by you through the purification process. I will explain more about the people that God placed in my path to help me through my healing process in more detail in later chapters, but it is important to note that God will not allow you to go through your healing process alone. He had Esther assigned a handmaiden that stood by her side. She was sent to help purify Esther. The handmaiden physically and spiritually helped to clean and purify Esther. She saw Esther in an intimate place in her humanness, her nakedness and she covered her. Who has God assigned to your life to cover you in your humanness and nakedness? Who can see you in your pain and still find the beauty beneath it and pronounce and prepare you to be the Queen whom God has called you to be?

He assigned men and women to my life to show me His love for me through their helping and loving hands. They led me from where I was to where God was placing and positioning me. God took me from bitterness and hurt and He positioned me as a wife and a daughter of God that is walking in her purpose. Esther had such a close relationship with her handmaidens that they knew who she truly was and that she was Jewish. Her chief handmaiden was even able to advise her on how to possibly save her people. God will give you people that will go through the purification process with you. They will see what others might see as flaws and love you despite that and show you God's love and direction for your life. They will walk you through the process and give you support and clarity on the direction that God is leading you. When I have been in turning points in my life, God would send those people that were assigned to my life to give me direction on my next step. You will know that these people are assigned to you from God because they will confirm the direction that God has given you in your quiet prayer time with Him, or God will confirm those things within your quiet time. To have good direction and understand the course of your life you must be willing to get before God and sacrifice your own will to hear clearly so you are able to move as a woman of purpose and faith.

This book will encourage you in your next steps for what God has for you and how to not be stifled by your pain but allow it to catapult you into purpose. God used my pain to allow me to reach out to other women who have been discouraged, abused, experienced self-hatred, rejection, loss, and trauma. I feel that God has allowed me to recognize it quickly in other women as I have experienced it within my own life. I have made it my mission to no longer be a hurt person that hurts people but a redeemed person that helps others become redeemed. Not only do I desire to be a person that redeems but also a person that helps others to be birthed into destiny and purpose.

Esther understood that her people had a destiny and purpose. She recognized that she had to sacrifice her own life and Queenship to save her people. When she became selfless, she found her true destiny and purpose. When we become selfless and relentless in our pursuit of God and what He has for our life, we will walk into our destiny. When we die to ourselves, we live. We must die to the pain and die to the old ideal of ourselves so that we may live and have purpose in Christ.

As you continue reading this book you will begin to identify how to be a person that moves from pain into purpose and how to move from ashes into being restored by God. You will be able to see how God uses His people and makes everything beautiful in His time. The process of pain allows you to know God and rely on His healing and purification. As you seek God relentlessly you will become a woman who walks in purpose and destiny. You will be a woman of prosperity, purpose, and you will understand the journey of going from pain to the palace. I challenge you to live fearlessly and full of faith and become a woman who is willing to be uncomfortable.

Who are you destined to save with what God has given you? You are made and created to solve a problem in the Earth and point others back to Christ. Let your life and process be a living testimony.

Chapter 2: The Pain

The pain, oh this is a place that I found so much comfort. I thought that pain was my identity. I thought that my life experiences only brought pain. How could I truly be loved and accepted? I was living a self-fulfilling prophecy of what I had spoken over myself for many years. As a prophet, I spoke death over myself, although I wanted more than what I was receiving. This pain was something that started within my childhood and I even believe it started at my conception. While my mom was pregnant with me, she had feelings of sadness as she did not want to bring another child into an unhealthy marriage. The devil used these feelings to make me feel rejected and unwanted. This feeling of being rejected followed me through my childhood since my parents were separated and got divorced while I was still at a young age. I longed for a father that was more present and validated my worth and my identity. When my expectations of a father's love were not met, I began to internalize many things and I believed that my father was not there because something was wrong with me.

I began to internalize the rejection. Not only did I feel rejected from my father; I also felt it from my classmates. I was diagnosed with a learning disability at a young age and the children would make fun of me for not being able to read. Not only did it take longer for me to understand things, but I was heavier than a lot of my classmates and would be teased for being fat. The devil used those feelings of rejection to confirm that I was not accepted and different. I began to feel that something was wrong with me. I thought that I was stupid and ugly. The boys would call me fat and dumb which reiterated that I was not able to receive love and acceptance because I was not smart enough or pretty enough. With not having a father present to validate me, I lacked what I needed to affirm who I was. I needed to be assured that I was loved and accepted. This led to me seeking validation, affirmation, and love in all the wrong places. This led me to dating a lot and my own feelings, thoughts, and emotions were a self-fulfilling prophecy as I was not receiving the love and validation that I craved for.

The mistreatment led to me becoming more desperate for love and feeling unloved. I was so detached from who God called me to be and who He said that I was. I was totally deceived by my own thinking. When I began to think of myself in the way that God sees me, the devil would bring up circumstances and my past to make me question who I was and if I were precious in God's sight. I wasn't aware that I was in a place that was filled with swine and that I had lowered my mindset to be eating among the pigs - although I am an heir of the royal priesthood. I began to eat the words, the mistreatment, abuse, toxic behavior, and being surrounded by people that did not respect themselves, respect others, nor respect God.

It was like being in a pig pen. A comfortable place. A place where I could wallow in my pain. A place where I found comfort in rejection, pride and in my own low mindset. I began to blame how I felt on others and not because of my own mindset. Just like the prodigal son, I moved away from good things and did not have the maturity to see the blessings and gifts right in front of me. My Heavenly Father was telling me to stop looking for a man's love and validation and seek Him instead. I wasn't ready to heed the warning that His love was enough for me. I lowered myself into the pig pen and ate with the swine. I thought I knew better than God. Instead of giving God my pain I decided to take these things into my own hands. The prodigal son asked for his inheritance when he was not ready to manage his inheritance and squandered it. Since he did not see the sacredness of his inheritance for his future, he squandered it on unnecessary things in the present.

I squandered how love should have been given and received. I mismanaged my purpose and my call. I did not see the purpose and call and how valuable it was. I was throwing my pearls among swine because I did not recognize that my pain was part of the path to purpose. I believed that my pain was a place where I should remain stagnant. I saw the words, negative treatment, and agreement by others who wore their pain as a badge of honor, as the slop that I was supposed to eat. I got comfortable in mess with negative and disrespectful people. I began to act like a pig because I saw myself as a pig. I thought that I didn't deserve more than dirt. When you play in slop and dirt expect to get dirt and mess on you, which makes you look like a pig.

When I felt low, I could have continued to be comfortable or I could choose to look up from the slop and realize that when I was in my Father's house and in safety, I did not have to live like this. Maybe my Father knows better than I do, and I should seek

His wisdom and guidance to see what He has for me. The prodigal son realized that his ways and his decisions were below his privilege.

I began to realize that, like the prodigal son, I was also living below my privilege. God has always seen me as royalty and a Queen. Esther was a woman that experienced loss and antisemitism. She was an orphan that was being raised in a time of turmoil. Her and her people were exiled from their home and in an area that they were despised for being Jews and were enslaved. She might have felt alone, lost, forgotten, and hated for who she was and where she came from. The way that Esther was treated before she became Queen could have made her feel that something was wrong with who she was and where she came from. We even see that Mordecai advised her to not let people know who and what she really was. At first, she agreed to hide her identity, but when she communed with Yahweh and sought His direction on what to do regarding the threat against the Jews, He had her expose who she truly was.

This choice could have cost her life and her people's lives. For most people, not dealing with the hurt, and not exposing the truth, your identity, and vulnerability seems more logical. With God you learn to take risks. You must take the risk of being transparent, vulnerable, and expose yourself so that you are able to find your new identity in God. This is the identity that you have always had but it was hidden behind the pain and loss that many people experience. When we have mistreatment, loss, trauma, and pain we begin to become a shell of ourselves. This is something that can make us shy away from destiny and understand the full potential that God has for us. When God has a great destiny for you, the devil will try to cause the things (and people) around you to make you feel less than what God has called you to be. This has been happening from the beginning of time. The serpent deceived Eve in two ways: one, he tricked her to believe what he said about her identity; and two, he misled her about the instructions that God had given Adam on eating from the tree. He made her think that she was not like God, although Adam and Eve were made in God's likeness. The devil will use this same tactic to this day. The devil made me think that I was not worthy of purpose and that God did not love nor care about me. This is contrary to all the things that the Bible states about who God is and how He feels about His children.

The way that I was treated made me feel and think that I was not worth it. Satan would send people that would fuel the rejection that occurred from the womb. Those that would speak against the Word of God would reiterate, "*You are not beautiful; you are fat, you are rejected, you are unloved, you are not important, you are not noticeable, and you serve no purpose.*" God had spoken the exact opposite to me. He told me that I was fearfully and wonderfully made, that I was the apple of His eyes; I am loved, redeemed, and restored. I was made with purpose, destiny, and made for greatness, and God designed my purpose while I was still in my mother's womb.

When I was in pain, I could not see that there was an escape route and that I was able to come out of the mess that my mindset and actions had placed me in. We must understand that as we move forward with intention, purpose will come from what we think and what we believe. We have the power to live out purpose and destiny or live in a defeated mindset. Some ways that we can change our minds about what we believe is to meditate on God's Word. When we focus on Him and His character it will make it harder to believe the lies that the devil will whisper to us. We will understand that God wants the best for us. We begin to see God's character and nature and we will allow Him to rule our lives. We should be so consumed with our relationship with God that it brings clarity to our lives.

When Esther faced the possibility that her people could be killed and annihilated, she had choices. She could have stayed in a place of pain, rejection, loss and sadness. She could have stagnated. Despite feeling all of these things she decided to seek God and His direction for her life. She set aside her own feelings, reached out to God in fervent prayer and fasting and asked others to come alongside her. During this time, she received confirmation that she was to go to the King, risk her life and save her people. What are some things that God is asking you to lay down? What hurt, feelings, insecurities, or rejections are you holding onto that God is asking you to lay down and trust Him to direct your path?

Many of us have allowed our feelings, actions, opinions, and decisions to dictate our lives. We make tough decisions about our lives based on our own minds, will, and emotions. We see that this can lead us to a pig pen. The prodigal son made decisions on the future of his life and inheritance. In his own pride he felt that he could do better, and he knew better than those that had greater wisdom and experience. His pride led him to the pig pen. If he had received his father's wisdom, he could have learned how to maintain an inheritance. His father would have directed him on his path toward purpose. Doesn't it make more sense for us to go to God than to make our own decisions?

When you are unable to understand your pain, predicaments, and life problems, you should seek the answer from God. We should seek to understand who we are, what we are purposed for, and the direction of our future from the God that created us. He knew you before you were in your mother's womb so He also knows your thoughts, will, emotions, and purpose. We must come into a place of submission and humility. We also must be willing to be transparent and honest.

God will be honest with you, but you must choose to be honest with yourself. The prodigal son got comfortable in his mess. He was tempted to eat from the pig pen along with the swine. At first, he wasn't honest with himself - that he was dirty, messy, and uncomfortable. At some point he began to look at his situation and realized that he was in a mess and living in a way that did not reflect where he came from. He realized that he came from privilege, but he was living a life of poverty. Are you living below your privilege? Have you become so comfortable in your mess that you've acted as a pig and allowed others to treat you as such? The question that you should ask yourself is: *"Am I allowing myself to stay in this situation, and to be treated like a pig?"*

In my life, I began to see that I was allowing myself to be treated less than I was valued. I began to realize that I desired to be treated a different way, and that I was living below my means. But how could I change it? Like the prodigal son, I began to see that this environment was one that I no longer wanted to be a part of, and I was available and willing to do better. Esther knew that she deserved to be treated better and so did her people. She decided to take a chance and make a decision that could make her new life uncomfortable or even end in death. Esther did not forget the mistreatment, pain, rejection, and abandonment that she felt in the past. She wanted to ensure that no one else would have to experience that through a wicked plot to annihilate her people. She remembered where she came from, sought God for a solution, consulted with Mordecai, and decided to move forward in what God had for her to save others from continual pain. God gave Esther and the prodigal son strategies to get out of their situations. In the case of the prodigal son, he was reminded that he had a father that kept him from the mess and by going home, he would continue to love and protect him. With Esther, she knew that she would need to go before the King unannounced, announce her true identity, and plead for his grace and mercy not just for herself but also for her people. Thankfully, she was successful in saving them.

We must be willing to see that for the problems, environment, mistreatment, and negative mindsets to change there had to be action and a made-up mind to end the stagnant state. There had to be a point where both people realized that there was a need for a change in mindset and be fed up with the situation around them. We must be able to recognize that there is a need for a change since this is the first step for us to act. The second act should be to pray for direction from God on how we should act and on when we should act. Timing is everything, and it should be used to determine our actions. If Esther had gone to the King at the wrong timing it could have cost her life, or it could have led to banishment. She was able to see the favor that God gave through her obedience even when she had every reason to fear.

There are things that God will do that will seem illogical to the human mind as "God hath chosen the foolish things of the world to confound the wise" (**1 Corinthians 1:27, KJV**). God has done this in my own life. He has tested my life and faith in ways where I had to sacrifice my own will for my life to desire what He had for me. I had to forget past people, friends, material items and go into new territory where I didn't know anyone and did not have any family. Would I be the person that would be like Abraham and go out into a new land and leave everything behind? I knew that my eyes would lead to a different life, but I could never imagine the abundance and fruitfulness that it would lead me to. When I was focusing on my pain and expected it to be my purpose, I did not expect greatness. When I started to walk in obedience to what God had called me to, I began to realize that there was more, and I could walk out of pain and walk into the palace. If I were to be a person that was focused on purpose, I could not focus on the past at the same time. I cannot go forward on purpose when I keep looking back at pain. You must look forward and move even when you are in pain and believe that your pain and your mess is not a place where you always have to reside.

If Esther were to look at her past, she would not have been able to unlock destiny. She understood the vital time and season and walked in it. Will you continue to look at the past, or will you recognize that this is an appropriate time? She even stated that, *"If I perish, I perish."* (**Esther 4:16, KJV**) What are you willing - or unwilling - to die to, or for? Are you willing to die to yourself to live the life that God has called you to? Living for God and moving forward into the unknown is not always easy but worth it. The unknown led to Esther being able to have favor, influence, and honor in the sight of the King. She saved her people, including her cousin Mordecai, and she was able to give wise counsel to the King.

One thing that stands out in this is that she was favored not only because she was beautiful but because of the way that she spoke to the King. She was a woman of character. She honored the King's role and position but still addressed her concerns and her fears. Will we be women who make excuses about our attitude because we feel justified in our pain? We need to be women of character and learn how much we need to purify our hearts and minds.

How do you speak to other people? Do you speak down to the people in your life? Are you a moral compass for others? Do people expect wise counsel and wisdom from you, and do you speak from a place of love when presented with tough situations? Will you speak out of bitterness or love? Esther could have spoken on behalf of her people and family and influenced the death of Haman. She allowed the King to come to his own conclusion, but she pointed out that Haman had plans to exterminate her people. Esther was vulnerable and honest and felt that she was in a place of safety. Her King made her feel safe when she went into the palace and pleaded the case of her people. He showed love and mercy.

God wants us to view Him as a place of safety. He wants us to lay in His lap and be vulnerable with Him. During this time, we will find healing and become greater women of character. When we are able to speak in wisdom and love, we are able to show growth and healing. We should be able to go to God with the same vulnerability as Esther. One thing that we see in Esther's circumstance is that she was a woman that went to God first and then she was able to be vulnerable with her husband. Many times, we think that our significant other or husband will be the first person that we need to get our healing from. We must realize that at times the only place where we can get true healing is from God. There are some wounds and pains that are so deep only God can repair it as He is our Creator and has known us before we were in our mother's womb.

God had me realize that I was a broken woman outside of His character. This was the day that God told me that He could not bless me with a husband because I would break him. Talk about a rude awakening! I thought that my attitude was in the right place and it was just everyone else around me that had a problem. In that moment I began to realize that I might need to change the way that I think, react, and treat people. Was I exemplifying the fruit of the Spirit, or was I a bitter woman that was subliminally/unconsciously pushing those that loved me away when I truly wanted people to stay? I was defensive, accusatory, angry, and bitter and had an attitude where I would hurt others before they could hurt me. I had a sharp and bitter tone with people. I would cut deep and in an undeserving way. I would wallow in my own pain and wasn't transparent with myself nor was I transparent with God. I looked for healing from my father or desired other men to validate me. I considered myself a loving person, but when I look back, I realize that I was acting as though I did not love myself and expected others not to love me. I realize now that I did not expect God to love me and I did not think of Him as a safe place. With my father not being as present as I needed, I did not feel that I could have a relationship with God as my Abba Father. I did not feel that I could lay in His lap and be transparent with Him. I questioned if I was worthy of love from anyone. I needed to go through a pruning process at the time of beautification. This was a process that needed to occur inside and out. I was angry and I was not a woman of character.

Then, I began to see that I wanted and needed to have a place of healing and I needed to go through a beautification process. The pruning and beautification process began when I became intentional about my process. When Esther was first presented to the King, she did not feel worthy to be considered a Queen. She knew that she was beautiful, but she was still dealing with some insecurities and was feeling unworthy. Many of us have found ourselves in situations, mantles, ministries, and positions that we did not feel worthy to carry, but that was God's way to push you through the process and get glory from your pain. Sis, He is using the pain to push you into the palace.

Esther had to spend a year in the palace in preparation. When Esther was in preparation, she went through a transition to become a woman of character. She had to look past her pain and come into the comfort of being in the palace. She had to come into a place that she knew she was worthy of the treatment that she was receiving in the palace. She was a woman of substance and character, and she was one that was becoming who God had called her to be. She was being processed. The process did not happen overnight. She had to get rid of unhealthy mindsets and coping mechanisms so she could go through her healing process. We must be willing to go through the process. We even see that in the time of growth and pruning of fruit. There is a specific time that we should be able to prune, pick, and allow the trees and our fruit to grow. A date tree has specific times and seasons where they are pruned, picked, and allowed to grow. It is a gradual process, and the process must occur in the right season.

Chapter 3: The Pruning

We must go through the pruning process. As we allow God to cut off the things in our life that are not like Him, we begin to change and grow. We will then begin to produce godly fruit and character. John 15 speaks about the pruning process, bearing fruit by abiding in Christ and having a relationship with God. His Word states, *"I am the vine, ye are the branches: He that abideth in me, and I in him, the same bringeth forth much fruit: for without me ye can do nothing."* **(John 15:5, KJV)** What abides in your life? What abides in your heart? What abides in your thought process? Does it glorify and abide in God or does it glorify and abide in your flesh and in your own worldly desires? John 15 also states that there is a time of pruning when God takes things that will not bear fruit and cuts them off. What is God trying to cut off from your life? There were many things that God needed to cut off from my life. God was showing me that there were many roots that He never intended for me to have in my life. I had roots of rejection, bitterness, self-hatred, low self-esteem, insecurity in who I was and whose I was, and I had no sense of purpose or importance. They were rooted in wrong mindsets and being around the wrong people reaffirmed my mindset with their treatment.

When I was playing with swine, I was expecting them to treat me as a pearl, but they treated themselves as pigs. You cannot expect a pig to act like anything but a pig. It is natural to have dirt, slop, and mess around you – just like pigs do. You may not understand that there is more than that in life. Without God's healing and guidance, dysfunction breeds dysfunction. When you have dysfunction as a normal part of your life, it can get passed down from generation to generation until someone has a spiritual and mental encounter where it does not have to continue and that that is the last generation that it will affect. This has been my story; I realized that the dysfunction that has occurred in my life and families' lives does not have to be passed down.

When Esther first went into the palace, she was entering unfamiliar territory. She was bringing in dysfunction, neglect, abandonment, and pain into the palace. It became a point that she had pain and problems that could keep her stuck in the past or she could release them and move into the present. I am sure that she realized that although she was going into unfamiliar territory, she was worth walking into her God-given destiny. She also had insightful and godly people around her to point her towards her destiny. Her cousin Mordecai was able to encourage her when he learned that she was part of the King's harem. One thing to remember is if she did not walk into her destiny, she would not have been able to save her people. She knew that to become everything that God was calling her to be, she would have to go through process and pressure. She had a choice to move forward and become all that God called her to be or to stay stuck in her past.

I had to learn this lesson. I had a lot of things in my past that kept me in bondage and in pain. Pain was my constant companion. I couldn't see what God was trying to do nor see myself going where He was trying to take me. I had lived in pain for so long and it kept me stagnant for years. Was I going to take on the pressure of the new to step into the palace? I began to see that I could not stay the same. The unknown was scary, but I was tired of the cycles that I was experiencing. I was able to see that staying in the pain was leading me to the pigpen. I was living out Einstein's definition of insanity where I kept doing the same thing over and over again while expecting a different result. I realized that to progress and grow I had to do things differently. I began to seek out ways to grow and heal. I began my healing process. I was once told that healing consists of a process where you are ripping off the band aid and feeling the unresolved pain once again. All the pain that I pushed down and suppressed was being bottled up and I felt pressured to confront it.

I used to be ashamed of everything. I lived in constant pain and allowed others to hurt me, but now I am no longer ashamed! I have let the bottled-up pain out and it made me into someone that was not afraid to confront my change. I started to see that my life was covered with pain, and I started to be around others that increased the pain. I started to realize that hurt people will continue to hurt people. God would not allow me to stay stuck in a place where I could no longer confront my pain. I started to see that God was allowing the pressures in life and other circumstances to help me see that I had to let go of that pain. He brought many people into my life that began to show me that I had to continually be aware of myself and how others treated me, whether it was good or bad. I realized that God would allow people to come into your life to help guide you into destiny whether it is by exposing your heart, loving you through a tough time, or by their actions that will give you the direction on where you should be going in life. When I decided to do some deep reflection, I realized I had a combination of all these things. I also realized that my journey was similar to Queen Esther.

Esther was pressured to push forward to destiny. She had pain and loss. Mordecai stood outside the palace as a guardian in her time that she was being developed as the potential to be Queen. He encouraged her to move forward into a new direction as he could see her potential when all she could see was pain. She was forced to leave what she knew, who she knew, and where she was located to come out of agreement with pain and familiarity. Sometimes God will have to get you into a place where you are uncomfortable, in unfamiliar territory, and have others around you see the potential in you to push you towards your next level in life. He will also allow some people to go on the journey with you. I started my journey of transformation where I was pressured into confronting myself and where I was. I was so hurt, and I was looking for love in all the wrong places. I wanted to be loved and I had forgotten who God had called me to be. I had fallen in love at a young age and thought that I would marry a particular man, but it did not work out. After this experience and loss, I was traumatized for years. I lost my ex-fiancée, my brother-in-law, and my great-grandmother in a six-month timeframe. I was told that I needed to be able to handle the grief and hold it together for everyone else. I was told that I had to be strong for my sister as she was grieving the death of my brother-in-law. My ex-fiancée was very close to my brother-in-law; and as we were both grieving the death of my brother-in-law, our relationship started to deteriorate. We both did not know how to grieve the loss and I was told that I had to be strong. Soon I realized you cannot allow others to dictate how you should process your own emotions. This can be stifling to your growth. I suppressed all this pain, and I was in a place of arrested development. I was stuck in a place of pain for eleven to twelve years and I would try to blame others for hurting me and I never really looked at myself. I realized that there was something wrong with me and I was carrying hurt. I also realized that for me to get something different, I needed to do something different. I decided to develop myself and start my beautification process. I changed my surroundings, the people I knew, and my mindset. I got under good training and met good people who started to lead me to my next purpose.

I was enrolled in an online marriage preparation course that made me confront my past and develop as a whole person in preparation for marriage. Esther was in a place of process and she was also part of a beautification process. God showed me that He was taking me through a beautification process and that He needed to prepare me for destiny and purpose. I was able to see that I needed an internal and external cleansing. I had been looking for love, validation, and healing from man and not from God. God began to show me that I needed to find that cleansing in Him.

Esther went through a process of beautification in which she took a year to learn how to prepare herself to be a wife, a woman of character, integrity, and a Queen in her own right. God took me through two and half years of testing and showed me who I really was. I began to see that I was a woman that was loved. I went from the mindset that I was not enough to a place where I was more than enough. During her beautification process, Esther was given a group of people (i.e., her handmaidens) that were going the same way as she was, and who would serve her and push her to where she believed she was going. God gave me a friend and a mentor that showed me how to embrace who God meant me to be, how to be obedient to God, walk out on faith and be willing to allow God to show His love through her. She made me a better person and spoke life into me. She was a woman of her word and a woman of character. She stretched me and molded me to become a better person and take me into my next place of destiny. She was able to show me that I was a person that could be loved by others and loved by God. I thought that I wasn't worthy of God's love and that I didn't deserve a great destiny. I remember one conversation where she treated me to get my nails done and told me that God was using her to prepare me for when my husband will do these things for me and that I did deserve these things. My mindset had me thinking that I didn't deserve love because of how I was treated, but I didn't realize that my mindset was why I was treated that way. If I didn't allow this treatment I would be treated like a queen, or I would remove myself from those who wouldn't respect me. She showed me how a godly woman should act and how to consult God on every part of my life. She was a person that helped to serve and guide me.

Esther was given a servant who assisted her. She guided her in the way that she could go, how to prepare to be a wife, and she also allowed her to be vulnerable. She was able to disclose her deepest secrets, including the fact that she was a Jew. She showed her who she was behind closed doors. Her servant did not judge her but understood where she was and assisted her in where she was going. The process will put pressure on you to become more. Esther was pressured into her purpose. She had gone through her beautification process. She realized that she had a voice and that she mattered, and what she had to say mattered. She realized that she had influence and character. She was given a platform that many did not have, and she needed to use her sphere of influence to not only to save herself but to save other people.

God had me go through this process as well. God put pressure on me to try to help others in the same way that my mentor had helped me. She helped me walk into new areas that I did not see as potential and that I could help other women just as she helped me. God called me into new territory to trust Him on a deeper level. Once I started my beautification process, He told me to pick out my wedding dress in faith. I wasn't in a relationship nor even engaged. A year and a half later I married the love of my life in that same dress. He told me to move to a new territory. To leave behind my government job that I had been in for four years to accept a position for a non-profit in which I had to raise a portion of my salary. He took me from something that looked stable to what could be an unstable situation. I know that Esther probably felt the same way when she was going into the harem. She knew her old place; it was familiar and secure. What if the King did not choose her? There was a chance that she would not be selected. After she was chosen as Queen and had to go before him to save her people, she wondered if the King would hear her request, or would he throw her out as it was against protocol to approach him unless he requested? She could have said that the King would banish her as he had banished Vashti. She still sought direction from God and went on a three-day fast and moved in the direction that God told her, despite the fear that she might lose her life. Her words were: *"If I perish then I perish."* **(Esther 4:16, KJV)**

I had some of these same doubts in my mind. Will I be able to sustain my income? Will I be able to raise all the funds to go into ministry? Why would I leave a stable job to go into something that is not guaranteed? Would I really be able to make an impact by ministering to these college students? I stepped out on faith and realized that all the answers were yes. By this time, I had moved to Kentucky where I only knew two people and I had no friends.

I had to uproot everything that I knew and become someone new. God showed me that I had to be able to change and move. I couldn't be the same broken person that I was. I couldn't stay with the person that didn't feel like I was enough. I had to embrace the new. I was moving into a new place, in a new apartment and I couldn't rely on my family to take me to the next level. I only had God to depend on.

Esther knew this as she was going into a palace where she was different, she didn't know anybody and had to trust God to protect her and guide her on becoming a wife. She was in a process of becoming. She was becoming a woman, she was becoming a Queen, she was becoming who God had prepared her to be. She didn't know what her preparation time would look like, but she knew that it was a new place for her new destiny. Life had to change to give her a new perspective.

These are all things that happened to me. God had to take me out of what I was used to and show me a new place. He literally took me to a University to guide me into purpose. I was walking in purpose and moving forward in destiny. He gave me an opportunity to walk with Him daily and show others how to be obedient and walk with Him daily. I realized that to step into what He called me, I had to be bold, brave, and obedient to do what He was telling me to do. I learned to prophesy and speak and pray into other people's lives no matter what others thought or felt. And you need people on your journey to help guide you. I had a dear friend that walked out being a woman of God and submitting to Him in all that she did, and not caring what others thought as she was being obedient to Him. This helped me step out in my journey and to be bold and brave because she showed me how to live courageously with God. I was able to inspire some of the college students with the way that I lived courageously and helped to disciple some students in their walk with God. Being a woman of character and living boldly for God is what led to me meeting my husband. While working for the campus God told me one Thursday that I should go out on campus and recruit and pray for students. It was that day that I was paired with a student that was involved with the campus ministry and was excited to share the gospel with others. This man was excited and had zeal and wanted others to know how God would change their lives. I did not know at the time that this man of God would be my husband. He was excited at the fact that I wanted to help others and show God to others. It was my godly character that made me stand out from the rest. This was what made Esther be distinct. She went through a pruning process and she was able to perfect what God had done in her. While she was secluded, she learned who she was, who God had called her to be, what God thought of her, her beauty in herself, her beauty in God, and how to exemplify that in her everyday actions. This is what prepared her to be chosen by God and be chosen by the King. To walk fully in purpose, we must understand why we are chosen.

Do you know why you were chosen? Do you know what He called you to do? I realized who God had called me to be. He showed me that in my own beautification process I learned who I was, what I needed to do, and who He called me to be. I realized that after I had gone through my healing process that I was able to overcome hurts, and I have a desire to see other women get healed and whole and walk into the purpose and identity that God had called them. I noticed that God would begin to send women in my life that needed guidance on what they should be doing, how to find out who they are in God's love, and that they were worth so much more than what they were settling for. I had to reflect on where I had come from and accept where I was going.

Esther was able to see that she was no longer a broken woman, but she had been given a voice to help and save others. God showed me that, just like Esther's pain, it wasn't for me, but it was to allow others to realize that they could overcome many things and they didn't have to be stuck in their past and they are able to step into their place of royalty. God wants us to know that we are ordained, called, and we are His chosen people. We are called a "royal priesthood." **(1 Peter 2:9 KJV)**

The day that I met my husband, he asked me if God had told me that "he was chosen." This was very impactful and made me reflect on when I knew I was chosen. I knew that I had a great impact to make but didn't know what that would look like. What did my own calling entail? I knew that my calling was bigger than just saving those that were in my close vicinity and my own family. I was called to save a nation. Esther knew that she was called to save not just her people but also a nation. This was a great responsibility; she realized that she was equipped and ready to do it. One of the first things that she did when she realized she was called to save her people was to do a corporate fast. This shows that we will need the support of God and others that have strong faith to move forward in what God has called us to do, especially if it is going to impact nations.

I realized that the Kingdom should be in support of one another as **1 Corinthians 12 (KJV)** says, we are one body with many functions. We must know how we fit into the body and that our function is vital and important. We see that our placement can make or break us. We must be where God has positioned us "for such a time as this," so that when He calls us to plead and petition for our people, we will be ready. Are you ready to go out, plead and stand in a gap for who God has called you to? Have you equipped yourself in a time of intimacy with the Father in a way that you would be able to move forward in this?

There were many times in which Esther stood in a place of intimacy with the Father. She was prepared. I had to learn that He will remove all other barriers and distractions that will keep us from focusing on Him. He removed my idol of marriage, my busyness, my friends, and everything I relied on to keep me from having to focus on my unhealed places. He made me go deep for Him to reveal what I needed to work on, and He changed me from the inside out. As I began to see why God created me, I realized that I was beautiful. He began to clean out the past hurt and emotional toxins from my heart. He also had me get rid of some of the physical toxins through detox baths and even took me to recipes of how Queen Esther would have eaten while in the harem to prepare to be Queen. This showed me that it is not only important to cleanse my heart but also be able to cleanse my body as well. God was trying to ensure that I was experiencing wellness in every way which would include mentally, physically, and emotionally.

Chapter 4: The Pressure

Cleansing was something that made me a better woman, but it was a process. Esther went through a cleansing process to ensure that she was made beautiful in her own time. **(Ecclesiastes 3:11, KJV)** She had to experience the pain, encounter God, and be open to change to move through the process. There was a point that I could see that my environment around me had to change for me to encounter myself and God in another way. I longed for change and wanted to move forward in purpose. There was a time that Esther could have felt these same feelings. Esther realized that she could no longer be that orphan as she was placed in an environment that forced her mindset to change. My environment changed, and I was able to see myself and God in a new light. When you are all alone, with no family, and not around anyone who is like you, you discover your secret place in God. Esther was a Jewish woman in a Persian world. She had left her cousin behind and didn't know anyone in the palace. This was my own environment when I relocated to Kentucky. I left all that I knew behind and I had to take my loneliness, sadness, fear, and other emotions to God. During those times I had to rely on God, and they were the most transformative moments of my life.

Esther was also transformed, and in process she would be in her secret time in prayer. In this time of prayer, she was taken through a process where she found out who she was and what God thought of her. In this secret place of prayer, she could lay down her insecurities and uncertainty. Will she be chosen by the King? Will he find out that she is Jewish? Will she have to deny her faith? These are thoughts that must have gone through her mind. Even when God gave her the mission that she should go before the King, she must have also felt that she heard wrong. *"Will he be willing to listen to me? Will my voice matter? Will I be killed? What will happen after I say what needs to be said?"* Although these were natural thoughts, her time, faith, and history with God allowed her to have faith in God and say, *"If I perish, I perish."* **(Esther 4:16, KJV).** Her history with God came through her time spent worshipping and connecting with God, and it matured her through her process. When you can see that God will be with you at your lowest points and your most vulnerable points, then you are able to know that He will care for you even during the most challenging and scary times of your life. Esther realized that God had protected her identity, and that He cared for her and allowed her to have favor. She trusted that if she and her people fasted, God would give her direction and protection before she came before the King. This means that you must be in full surrender and be willing to sacrifice to receive the next direction for your life. Your sacrifice could save nations. Esther was willing to surrender her life for God's purposes. Have you gotten to the point that you can say I am willing to give my life to fulfill the purpose that You have for me in life? I have learned that no matter the stakes, it is worth being willing to sacrifice all.

There was a time that I gave up a secure job with benefits to take a job where I had to fundraise. Many people could not understand why I would go into a place of insecurity and I would leave everything I knew to go into a place where I was not comfortable. I learned that in insecurity and in the unknown, God has an opportunity to show up. When you are in an unknown place with God, it gives you a chance to truly surrender and trust the process. Esther knew from her past relationship with God that she could trust Him. She trusted Him in the process. The process is a time of growth and transformation. When you are in a time of insecurity, God shows Himself as someone that you can trust. Knowing this about God gives you hope and encouragement. In my process I was able to talk about my pain with Him and heal from the past. This process began when I was learning that my past pain could no longer define me, and I should begin to love myself the way that God loves me. I began to see where He said that *"I was fearfully and wonderfully made"* (**Psalms 139:14, KJV**) and He knew me before I was formed in my mother's womb. (**Psalms 139:13, KJV**) He knew me, He defined me, and He called me to purpose. I began to see that I could no longer stand back and think that I didn't have greater worth, as He made me for purpose. I began to see that God wanted to use me for a greater purpose when He gave me the opportunity to be an Associate Director of a Campus Ministry. I didn't think that I had enough experience to be a leader and mentor to others because in the midst of my life I had forgotten that I had a significant voice. Many times, I experienced things to make me think that my voice didn't matter, or my experiences did not matter. As I was helping younger women and advising them on life and experiences, I realized that my voice was important, and it can help and heal others.

As we observe Esther's life, we notice that she probably felt unsure and wondered whether her voice mattered or if she had influence. Over time, when she was in the harem and going through her process, she began to find her voice. She learned that there was a time and a moment that her voice would matter and that she would need to speak *"for such a time as this."* **(Esther 4:14, KJV)** A woman of impact knows when to speak and when to be quiet. She knows her influence and impact and doesn't have to continually speak, but she should speak "the Word of the Lord" when the presence of God comes upon her. Esther learned that speaking with grace and at the right timing allowed her to be heard and it changed the perspective of others and changed the course of their lives. She was a woman of self-discipline, and she learned how to be proactive and not reactive. She was a woman that began to pray in difficult situations and not allow her emotions to overcome her. She went to God, told Him about her concerns and acted on the direction that He gave her after seeking His face. As women of God, we must tell God about our concerns even when we are emotional and allow Him to give us perspective and direction and when to act.

Esther also had to have the character to back up her words. If she had a wrong attitude, she could have been banished just like Vashti, the former queen. When Esther walked in integrity and grace, that allowed people to trust what she said. I realized that the reason that I was not effective in ministry at one time was because I was broken. When you are not willing to be processed and you are in a place of brokenness you will bleed on those that did not break you. There is a healing process that a person must go through so that they are effective in ministry. When you become processed, you can push forward and be blessed for ministry. When you overcome brokenness, you can help others come out too. Like that saying goes "hurt people hurt people," but we must remember that "restored people can restore people." We should be in a place of restoration where we can also get others restored. Esther was able to speak to the King in a place of honor and respect, and the King saw her character. Esther was able to speak truth in a way that he would listen. She was given influence in the decisions of the edicts that the King would declare.

What is the process that God is trying to take you through? Are you allowing God to take you through the process, or are you avoiding it? If I avoided the process, I was not able to grow or move forward. I stayed stagnant for years because I was not willing to take an introspective look at myself and see that I was wounded. When I began to allow God to speak into my life, He showed me my brokenness and how I can move forward with life. He allowed me to see my broken experiences through His perspective and why I experienced things that had nothing to do with me, but they were other people's actions and that those experiences did not have to define me. I lived through my experiences; they made me a better person. The Prodigal son went through many experiences that were beneath his status, but it did not mean that he was less than his status. His experiences made him realize who he was and whose he was and realize the importance of his identity and where he came from. It is important to know where you came from and where God is trying to take you. Esther realized through healing who she truly was, and she became aware of the identity that God had established through her.

I have seen this in my own life; I was a person that was full of pain and brokenness, and once I began to process the pain, I realized that I was called to help women walk in purpose and identity while overcoming pain. I realized that I had gone through many things and that I have been able to bounce back, and like a Phoenix I was able to rise above the ashes. A Phoenix is a mythical creature, but God was showing me that even if they were burned, they always came back to life. It is like Shadrach, Meshach, and Abednego. They were placed in the fiery furnace and were able to come out unscathed. **(Daniel 3, KJV).** Although there are painful experiences that seem like they were sent to kill you, they will make you stronger and you will come back more resilient and fuller of life, and you will know who God has called you to be. When you can go through the process of the furnace, God will allow you to feel the heat, but He will protect your life. You will be a testimony, that you lived through the pressure and the process.

I realized that there is power in my mouth and power in my story. Your pain is your story. Your pain is the time that you are being burned to the point that you thought it was ashes, but God restored you into something that you never thought you could be. I never thought that I would mentor women and speak life into broken places. This was never a thought, because I believed that I had to live in a place of pain for the rest of my life. I realized that I had to love myself enough to want to overcome my situation - and then I was able to really embrace the process and move into a healthy place. I realized that embracing the process would allow me to be perfected in Christ and become the woman that he had fashioned and designed me to be. Through my journey I realized that He makes everything beautiful in His time. **(Ecclesiastes 3:11, KJV).** God gave me beauty for my ashes, and He allowed me to become a Phoenix that rose above the ashes. I became a restored woman who realized I was royalty and that I was chosen by God. He allowed me to arise and begin to walk in my purpose "for such a time as this."

Accepting the process can lead to God's perfection.

Chapter 5: The Perfection

"And He said unto me, My grace is sufficient for thee: for my strength is made perfect in weakness. Most gladly therefore will rather glory in my infirmities, that the power of Christ may rest upon me." (**2 Corinthians 12:9, KJV**) We see in this scripture that God can use our pain to push His power so that we become more powerful with God. We see that when Esther was at her most desperate point and thought that all would be lost for her people, God was able to use her as a vessel and a mouthpiece to save them. When we realize that we are in desperate situations and feel that we are in the depths of despair, we come to God. He can turn our desperate situations in our favor. When Esther was in a place of full surrender, God took control and gave her favor. When we embrace the process, we can see God's perfection. *"His strength is made perfect in our weakness."* We must remember that perfection comes when we enter an intimate place with God and be transparent about our weakness and admit that we need Him to survive – and thrive.

Esther was able to convey this in a literal sense when she had to come to God on behalf of her people and plan a strategy to save her people and nation. What are some things that you need to be transparent about so God can perfect you and give you strength? I realized in my most desperate and broken moments where I had nowhere to turn and was in complete vulnerability, I had to turn to God. In these moments I was able to find strength and find my full identity. When I was able to give God my perspective and see things from His perspective, I was able to process and grow. I saw that I could use the hurtful and challenging things in my life to push me to be a better woman. I was persistent and an overcomer. I learned that I didn't have to be defeated but I could move forward with the help of God. God showed me that there was purpose in the painful experiences. The purpose was to use that same pain and experiences to save a nation of broken people. It made me realize that the same pain that I was experiencing, others are experiencing it as well. I could be a source of hope and allow them to see that they did not have to stay in a place of pain and feeling that there is nothing that they could do. They could also participate in their own healing process. I learned that you must be a willing participant in your own healing process and in being transparent with yourself and others. When I was willing to address the burns and see them as a lesson then I was able to move forward and be restored and regenerated just like a Phoenix. I went in the fire, but it wasn't able to consume me. The fire allowed me to soar and be all that God had called me to be. I realized that I was not supposed to stay stuck in my pain, but I was meant to deliver people from pain. I realized that when I abide in Christ, I can move forward in the purpose that God has for me. It is a place of walking in His perfection. (**2 Corinthians 12:9, KJV**)

Where I felt like I was not worthy, God began to perfect those things that concerned me; He showed me that I am worthy, and I was called to save a nation. (**Esther 4:16-17, KJV**) I realize that I was called for such a time as this and that I did not need to fear what He has assigned to me. I realized that it was okay to take risks in His direction. It was okay to move forward in what He had called for me to do, no matter what others would say. He showed me that I would relocate and meet my husband within 6 weeks of getting there (which I did, we met 6 weeks and three days after I relocated), that I would have the funding for my job which came from an unexpected place and a stranger, and that I would continue missions work in Cuba - all in the same year. All these things were given to me by His direction. Some felt that I was crazy and not hearing correctly or I was moving too fast, but when the hand of God is directing you, you will know when to move forward and move in "such a time as this." *Such a time as this* is a time that God will give you direction to move forward - in His "perfect" time. God's time is beyond what the human mind can grasp. It is "Kairos" time, which is the opportune time and moment, also known as "God moments." (**Webster Dictionary**)

These God moments will lead to your process of saving a nation and walking in purpose. There comes a time in your life when you must be able to decide that you are willing to be the change that you want to see. There are times in our lives that we can see a problem that we know needs a change, but we might feel that we are not capable of being the change that needs to occur. We must be willing to see that God might have put this problem on our heart to make the change. When we allow God to guide us then we will be able to discern the "Kairos" time within our own life. In the uncertainty of the unknown God can make Himself "perfect in our weakness." When one becomes humble, submitted to God, and obedient with a pure heart it can lead to transition into the palace.

Chapter 6: The Palace

The palace was a place that was looked upon with fear and new territory for Esther and Mordecai. In the beginning, it could have been a place of ashes or mourning. Esther and Mordecai could feel that this was a place that could lead to the loss of their people. It even led Mordecai to mourn and put on sackcloth and ashes, not realizing that this same place would be where his promotion would occur. The promotion and assignment were given by God. Esther and Mordecai's faithfulness to God led to favor. Mordecai's willingness to reveal the plot to kill the King led to his promotion. It is a reminder to us that the good deeds that you have done are not overlooked by God and He will reward your obedience and faithfulness.

It is also important to understand the timing that you are in. We see that Mordecai approached it as a time of mourning; but God used the time as an opportunity to show up, guide Esther on her next steps, and define her purpose and destiny to save her people and promote Mordecai to his next assignment. It is also ironic that Mordecai saves the King's life, and the King made the decision to save Mordecai's life. We might face hard decisions and see that people are against us, but God will look for you to be obedient no matter how it makes you feel. I have had circumstances in my own life where God has made me pray for and minister to people that have offended and hurt me and did not have my best interest at heart.

To be promoted and to get to the palace, you must be willing to see people the way that God sees them, even if they do not treat you the same way. We must live out the principle of loving your enemies as you love yourself. **(Matthew 5:44, KJV)** The palace is one way to help you see things from a higher perspective. You can come into a new environment and a new thought process. When you get to the palace, you begin to see who you are and who you are called to be. You will understand your influence and purpose. You have a new way of living and confidence in where you are going. Esther began to see that she was a woman of influence and that her husband was willing to listen to her. She was able to test this when she went to beg for the lives of her people and then arrange a meeting with the King, herself, and Haman. She realized that she was trusted and considered a woman of favor and influence. She has gained the place and position that she was in and began to realize that she was there because God had a plan for her life.

I looked at Esther's life and it helped me understand the things that occurred in my own life. I saw that the pain and struggles that I experienced were leading me to the palace and into purpose. I began to see that the process that God was taking me through was to assist me with being healed and whole and to help with new ideas, concepts, and mindsets. I was moving towards purpose. My physical move to Kentucky changed my perspective and allowed me to realize that I had so much to offer hurting women and others that want to know who and what God had called them to. I realized that moving from all that was familiar changed my perspective and helped me to begin to see myself and others the way that God sees them. The palace was a place of understanding that who you are, your influence, and character can help save a nation.

Do you know where you stand in the palace? Do you understand your influence? Do you understand that what you have to say matters? Many times, I felt that my voice was insignificant because I said the things that were needed to be said, but it made others uncomfortable. I hated that I thought differently, but God began to show me that He gave me a unique voice to meet the unique needs of people that had similar experiences. Many women have felt alone and that their voice did not matter, as it hasn't fit into the culture and they've felt the need to assimilate. Even Esther hid her voice at first and then changed to understand that her voice had influence as a Jewish woman and that she didn't have to die for being who she was. She had the confidence to finally say, *"I am a Jewish woman living in a place that is looking to destroy me and my people."* Can you stand in the face of persecution and still be the person that God has called you to be? The palace is a great place to be. It is the place where you are guided by God, and you know who you are. The process of getting to this place is hard, and it can be a beautification process and the purification of your mind, body, soul, and spirit. It is allowing the cleansing from God and the Holy Spirit and no longer relating to yourself as a broken person that has trauma but seeing yourself as the healed person that God has called you to be. I stopped seeing myself through a broken lens but instead I started seeing myself as a healed person and a part of God's inheritance and royal priesthood. We should be willing to change our garments from common wear to our royal garments. This is taking off poverty mindsets. We must remember God's promises; He says who we are. We should not believe the lies that can come from hurt and trauma. Trauma and pain will distort vision, but God can clarify vision. Be open; see yourself through God's lenses. He will take you into places you never expected.

There are times that God has led me to great places of uncertainty which led to my growth and strengthen my faith. I noticed that the more that God puts on my heart to be faithful and trust Him, the greater we have been blessed. I have been reflecting on living through the 2020 Pandemic. Many have experienced loss due to Covid-19, but with God's direction we have prospered. God led us to buy a home right in the middle of the pandemic and we see the favor on our lives because we were willing to trust His direction and follow His commands. My husband and I reflected on how we followed God's voice and God accelerated what we have been able to do in a little bit of time. In less than two years of being married we have seen God prosper us in magnificent ways. We even see this in the story of Esther.

We must remember that our pain can push us into purpose and although we may feel as if we are being burned, like the Phoenix we can be restored and come back better than ever. God never intended for us to be in a place where we are continuously mourning in sackcloth and ashes, but He will use these times to promote us into position. It is a reminder of what God can do. We are reminded of what God can do through **Romans 8:18 (KJV)** which states, *"For I reckon that the sufferings of this present time are not worthy to be compared with the glory which shall be revealed in us."* God wants our suffering to be used to be a living testimony to others. In my life I have survived many obstacles. These experiences equipped me to be a glorified vessel for God's use. I realized that the experiences were to glorify God's process and what He can make out of us. When we are willing to be on the anvil and be refined into the tool that He has created for us, we are able to save a nation and be an example to those that feel they must stay in their situation. Once we get to the palace, we can lead others there too.

We must embrace our pain and move past it. We should be willing to be transparent with our identity and our story so that we are able to assist others with their own breakthrough. Esther was able to be transparent with the King and let him know about her needs and her love for her people. When she was transparent and humble, the King was able to see her heart and honor her wishes. With her transparency she was able to save her people. Are you willing to be transparent with those that God has told you to tell? Are you ashamed of who you are and what you have been through, or are you willing to be transparent to see other people receive breakthroughs? It was important that we see beyond ourselves and say, "if I perish, I perish" and lay down our pride to ensure that we can save a nation.

Being a part of the palace is also the idea that you are willing to help others and be confident in the position that you are in within the palace. The palace is a place where you can advance and grow in many areas; you can remain in communion and continue to be guided as purpose and position will change throughout the years. As the Queen was able to learn through her time of leadership, we will also grow and learn and process our identity and purpose. We will be called to different things at different times. We must remember that who we are will solidify our purpose. Pain will always have a purpose and you don't have to stay in a place of being burned or dead, but you can be restored and used for the purpose that God has for you. You will be the Phoenix that arises from the ashes. You will not have to stay in mourning and God will use those times to catapult you into destiny.

Conclusion

There are times in our life that we experience a lot of pain, even from a young age, so that we feel that it would keep us from walking into the destiny that God has for us. We must realize that we have to change our environment, relationships, and mindsets to push us from staying in our past so we can transition into new territory and purpose. We must recognize that there will be pain, pruning, process, and perfection to get to the palace. Healing is a process. We must recognize our identity and find out who God calls us to be. This requires a level of intimacy with God and His Word to see His character and how we reflect Him as we have been made in His image. We all grow and develop through purification and process. It is not until we are able to reflect on our pain that we are able to begin to walk in purpose and destiny. Esther was afraid to go away from all that she knew. Once she was in the beautification process, she had to shift her ideas to prepare for where she was going and to develop into the Queen that she was preparing to be. There will be a time when you will be prepared for the future and given a chance to walk in it. Life can bring unexpected things your way, but if you are willing to take these things in stride and know that you will be guided through your life and discipleship with God, you will know that you will be fully secure even in an insecure situation. Remember that God will never leave you or forsake you **(Hebrews 13:5, KJV)**.

The more stability that you experience in your relationship with God, you will also have stability and security in your identity and purpose. When you communicate and have stability with God, He will begin to reveal the purpose that He had created you to be. You have to be able to understand that your purpose will be tied to the thing that you will wake up thinking daily on how you can make a difference by doing it. I naturally have the desire to see women come from a place of pain to a place of positivity in who God has created her to be, and that her pain can be processed in a healthy way to overcome obstacles. Her developed character and beautification will speak to her level of influence and change her atmosphere and the people that she is called to save.

CPSIA information can be obtained
at www.ICGtesting.com
Printed in the USA
BVHW091317080421
604490BV00006B/316